PianoTrainer Series

The Foundation Pianist Book 1

A technical and musical curriculum
for pianists at post Grade 1 level

Karen Marshall & David Blackwell

FABER MUSIC

Contents

Acknowledgements

Many thanks to all of Karen Marshall's pupils who have learnt and commented on the music, and to the teachers who have given feedback.

Karen would like to dedicate her work to the late Christine Brown, who did so much for her understanding of teaching piano technique.

With many thanks to Lesley Rutherford for her care and attention on the manuscript.

© 2018 by Faber Music Ltd
This edition first published in 2018
Bloomsbury House, 74–77 Great Russell Street, London WC1B 3DA
Music processed by Jackie Leigh
Text designed by Susan Clarke
Cover design by Adam Hay
Printed in England by Caligraving Ltd
All rights reserved

ISBN10: 0-571-54065-1
EAN13: 978-0-571-54065-5

To buy Faber Music publications or to find out about the full range of titles available please contact your local music retailer or Faber Music sales enquiries:
Faber Music Ltd, Burnt Mill, Elizabeth Way, Harlow CM20 2HX
Tel: +44 (0) 1279 82 89 82   Fax: +44 (0) 1279 82 89 83
sales@fabermusic.com   fabermusicstore.com

Introduction

The Foundation Pianist is a set of two books for students who are past beginner stages and who want to develop a technical and musical foundation in order to progress to the intermediate stages of playing.

This book includes five chapters that can be studied over a few months. Each chapter explores a different piano technique through a variety of elements, including a daily exercise, a sight-reading piece and repertoire by the great composers alongside newly written educational music. There's also an exciting section called 'Musical time travel' that takes the player on a journey to different musical periods of the past and introduces them to the style of that time. *The Foundation Pianist* not only develops students' technique, reading, theory and musicianship, but also provides an insight into the world of classical music, from madrigals to symphonies, and from operas to concertos.

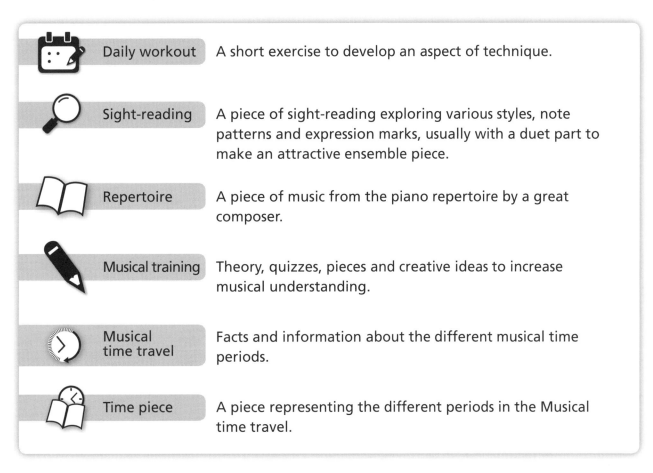

Daily workout	A short exercise to develop an aspect of technique.
Sight-reading	A piece of sight-reading exploring various styles, note patterns and expression marks, usually with a duet part to make an attractive ensemble piece.
Repertoire	A piece of music from the piano repertoire by a great composer.
Musical training	Theory, quizzes, pieces and creative ideas to increase musical understanding.
Musical time travel	Facts and information about the different musical time periods.
Time piece	A piece representing the different periods in the Musical time travel.

Our aim is to help develop a generation of pianists who understand basic piano technique and the musical time periods of the pieces they are playing. We hope you enjoy the journey and the music making within these pages.

Karen Marshall and David Blackwell

Musical sentences

phrasing, legato *and the use of dynamics*

A **phrase** is like a musical sentence. Imagine a singer taking a breath before each new phrase. Phrases (or slurs) should be played *legato.* Often phrases are shaped by a *crescendo* and then a *decrescendo.*

 Daily workout

Long and Short Phrases

Karen Marshall

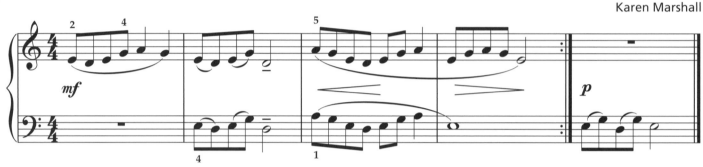

 Musical training

Listen to your teacher play the sight-reading piece below. Using your finger in the air (drawing in a rainbow shape), can you show the phrasing? How are dynamics used?

 Sight-reading

Loch Lomond

Play your part an octave higher when playing as a duet.

Scottish traditional
Arr. David Blackwell

Quasi Adagio

(20th century)

- Record yourself playing the first two left-hand chords over and over. Using the notes A B C D E (the first five notes of the A minor scale), improvise your own melody above these recorded chords.

- Practice tip: before you play, identify all the phrases, noticing their different lengths.

Béla Bartók (1881–1945)

Our Song

Can you spot the phrase patterns in this piece? How many bars are in
each phrase? Some of the musical words, symbols and notes have boxes
alongside them – can you write in the note names and explain the words
and symbols in the boxes?

David Blackwell

1 Name the notes with boxes above or below them in these tunes.

2 Play each melody. Where do you think the phrase marks should go? Can you draw them in?

3 Add some dynamics to the music and write what they mean below.

p _____   *mf* _____

mp _____   *f* _____

crescendo _____   *decrescendo* _____

Jeremiah, Blow the Fire

Rocky Mountain

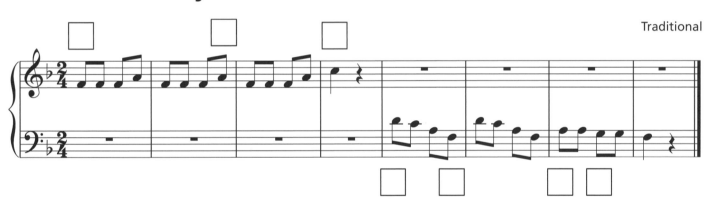

One Little Candle

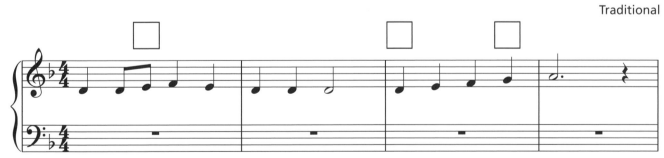

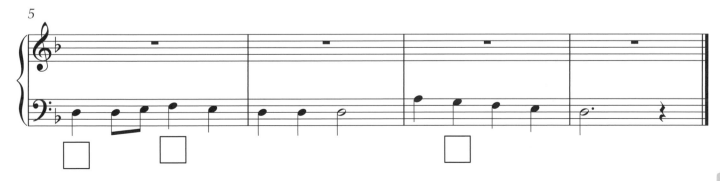

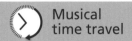
The Renaissance period

(about 1400–1600)

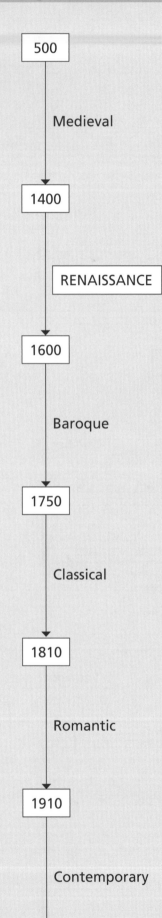

500

Medieval

1400

RENAISSANCE

1600

Baroque

1750

Classical

1810

Romantic

1910

Contemporary

Look up the highlighted words to see what they mean.

A lot of music from this period was written for the church, including masses, motets and **anthems**. The style was **polyphonic** (= 'many sounds'), which means the music was built from a number of different musical lines that fitted together (unlike, say, a melody and accompaniment). Song styles included **madrigals**, that often used a technique called **word-painting**. A very important collection of nearly 300 keyboard pieces from this time was the *Fitzwilliam Virginal Book*. Music was usually written in **modes** – these were like the scales we use today but each had a different sequence of tones and semitones. For example, the Aeolian mode uses the notes A B C D E F G A.

Composers: John Dunstable, Josquin des Prez, William Byrd, Thomas Tallis, Palestrina, Lassus, Giovanni Gabrieli, John Dowland

Instruments: cornett, trumpet, **sackbut** (brass), **viols**, lute (strings), recorder, **rackett** (wind), virginals (keyboard), tambourine, tabor or drum (percussion)

Online listening

Find an example of these instruments playing and circle the words that describe them:

- **Sackbut**   rich   mellow   airy   loud   soft

  What modern instrument beginning with T is this like?

  _____

- **Viols**   thin   tinny   quiet   spikey

  What modern instrument beginning with V is this like?

  _____

Listen to these Renaissance pieces. Can you write a word to describe their character?

- Orlando Gibbons, *Hosanna to the Son of David*: an anthem in polyphonic style.

  Character _____

- Thomas Weelkes: *Since Robin Hood*: a madrigal – listen for the word-painting at 'to skip'.

  Character _____

- Michael Praetorius, *Terpsichore*: a collection of over 300 instrumental dances. Choose one to listen to.

  Character _____

The Carman's Whistle

(Renaissance period)

In the Tudor period, a carman was a person who moved goods by horse
or cart – whistling was a way of managing the horses. William Byrd's
variations on this tune were printed in the *Fitzwilliam Virginal Book*.

Tudor song
Arr. David Blackwell

2 Finger workouts
even finger work, patterns and shapes

Even finger work – when the notes are all the same length and in time –
can be difficult to achieve. You need to **1** Listen to keep your playing even,
and **2** Practise to develop strong enough fingers.

 Daily workout **For Even Fingers**

Carl Czerny (1791–1857)

 Musical training

Mark an accent in pencil on the first note of every group of ♫♫♫♫ (as bar 1),
then play with the accents. Record yourself – is your playing even?

 Sight-reading **Secret Agent**

David Blackwell

Duet
part

The Hunt

(Romantic period)

Broken chords/arpeggios use the 1st, 3rd and 5th notes of a scale.
Fill in the missing letters of the C major arpeggio and broken chord:

• arpeggio: C   E   _____   C

• broken chord: C   E   G   E   _____   C   G   _____   E   C

Cornelius Gurlitt (1820–1901)

Piano*Trainer*

Musical training

The major scale generator

Using this scale generator, create the scales of C, G, D, A and F major.

Name of scale _____

STEP 1

From the musical note names (A–G), select the notes in the correct order for the scale you want to play. Start with the key note and write them in these boxes (one or two octaves):

STEP 2

The pattern of tones (T) and semitones (ST) for the **major scale** is:
T T ST T T T ST

Check your letter names above – have you used the right pattern? Add any sharps or flats you need in the boxes. Play your scale through to check that it sounds right.

STEP 3

Write the letter names of the scale on the keyboard below, including any sharps or flats. Remember to check you have the correct pattern of tones and semitones.

Right-hand fingering:

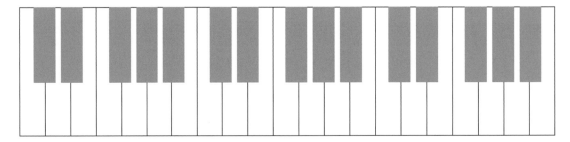

Left-hand fingering:

STEP 4

Work out the correct fingering – ask your teacher to help if necessary – and add the finger numbers to the keyboard above. Work out where your thumb goes first.

Common finger patterns

Right hand 1 2 3 1 2 3 4 1 2 3 1 2 3 4 5   1 2 3 4 1 2 3 1 2 3 4 1 2 3 4

Left hand 5 4 3 2 1 3 2 1 4 3 2 1 3 2 1

Karen Marshall

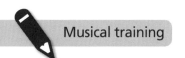

Musical patterns

Spotting patterns in music can really help music reading and speed up learning a new piece. The piece below includes lots of musical patterns. See if you can spot the following, and mark them in the music. (A sequence is where the same pattern is repeated on higher or lower notes.)

(Repeat of the melody line) (G major triad) (A minor triad) (a four-note sequence)

(The first 5 notes of D minor, descending) (The first 5 notes of C major, descending)

Menuet in A minor

(Baroque period)

from Partita No.6

Johann Krieger (1651–1735)

The right-hand mordent or trill in bars 7, 15 and 23 can be played like this:

Add your own dynamics. Composers often left these to the performer in the Baroque period.

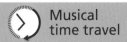

The Baroque period

(about 1600–1750)

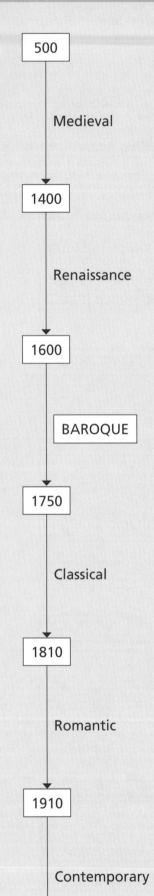

500

Medieval

1400

Renaissance

1600

BAROQUE

1750

Classical

1810

Romantic

1910

Contemporary

Look up the highlighted words to see what they mean.

Baroque music was composed in major and minor keys rather than modes. The bass line was provided by the **basso continuo**, played by harpsichord or organ and bass instruments like the cello, double bass or bassoon. The keyboard part also played chords using a **figured bass** – numbers below the bass notes indicating the chords to play. Music was often **contrapuntal** – the **fugue** was an important contrapuntal form. The Baroque period saw the rise of the solo concerto and **concerto grosso**. Other important forms were **dance suites**, **oratorios**, cantatas and operas. Music was often decorated with a lot of ornaments – trills, turns and mordents.

Composers: J. S. Bach, George Frederick Handel, Domenico Scarlatti (all born in 1685), Henry Purcell, Georg Philipp Telemann, Antonio Vivaldi, François Couperin, Johann Pachelbel

Instruments: **harpsichord**, organ (keyboard), violin, viola, cello (strings), flute, oboe, bassoon (woodwind), trumpet, trombone, cornet (brass), timpani (percussion)

Online listening

Listen to these pieces and write a word to describe their character.

- Handel, *Zadok the Priest*: an anthem for voices and instruments written for the coronation of King George II in 1727.

  Character _____

- Vivaldi, *The Four Seasons*: a set of four violin concertos exploring the characteristics and moods of spring, summer, autumn and winter. Choose any movement.

  Character _____

- Pachelbel, *Canon*: a contrapuntal piece built on a repeating bass line, played by the basso continuo group at the start.

  Character _____

Time piece

Allegro

(Baroque period)

This is the opening of the first movement of Bach's Concerto in E major
for violin and orchestra. Bach also arranged it later as a harpsichord
concerto. Can you spot the repeating musical patterns in this piece?

J. S. Bach (1685–1750)
Arr. David Blackwell

Articulation activation

and couplet slurs

Articulation marks change the way notes should be played. Here are some examples:

legato
notes joined together

staccato
notes detached

accents
with force

 or

sforzando
with force

tenuto
with weight

 Daily workouts

Staccato and *Legato*

Do this exercise *slowly* hands separately and together, *legato*, *staccato* and *forte* and *piano*.

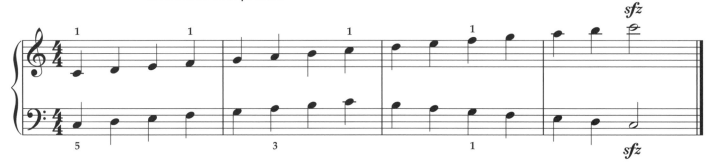

Articulation Workout

Karen Marshall

Rocking (couplet slurs)

Karen Marshall

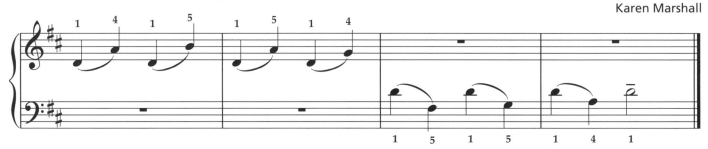

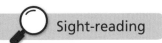

Trampoline

Count carefully in your head to make sure you put in all the rests.
Listen to your teacher play this first, clapping three beats in the bar
and stressing the first. Look out for the different articulation marks.

David Blackwell

With a confident bounce

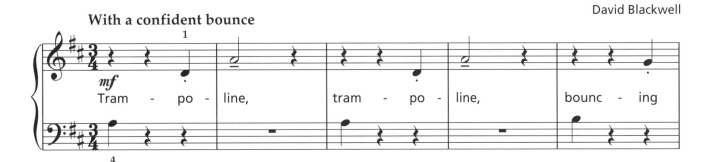

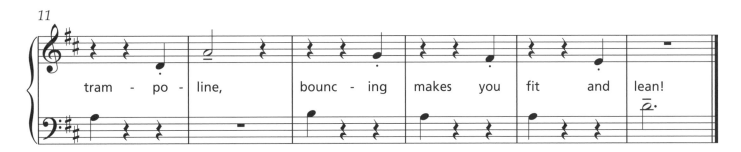

Duet
part

With a confident bounce

 Musical training

Write the following on the stave below:

1 A one-beat note with a *staccato* marking

2 A four-beat note with a *tenuto* mark

3 ♫♫ with a slur over the top

4 A two-beat note with an accent mark

5 ♫ with a couplet slur above, and a *sforzando* on the second note

Ecossaise

(Classical period)

Find out what an Ecossaise is. Spot the following intervals in the music:

Minor 3rd: bar _____   Perfect 5th: bar _____   Perfect octave: bar _____

Ludwig van Beethoven (1770–1827)

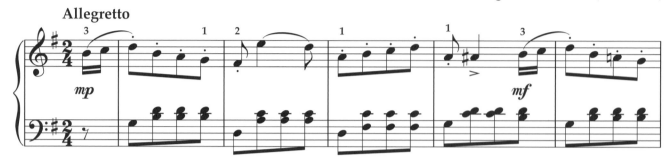

Musical training # Articulation

Add some articulation to the music below – some ideas are given in the first line. It's from a set of variations Mozart wrote on the tune 'Ah! Vous dirai-je, Maman' ('Ah, shall I tell you, mother'), well known as the tune to 'Twinkle, twinkle, little star'. When you've finished, play it through, following all the articulation you've added.

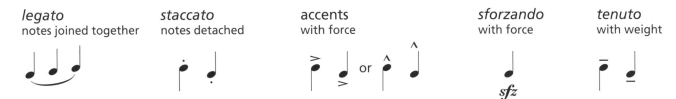

legato
notes joined together

staccato
notes detached

accents
with force

sforzando
with force

tenuto
with weight

French Folksong

Arr. W. A. Mozart (1756–1791)

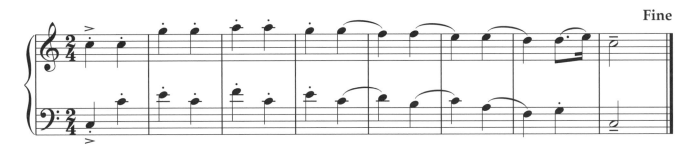

 Musical training ## Rhythms

1 Clap the ten rhythms below, counting four beats as you clap:

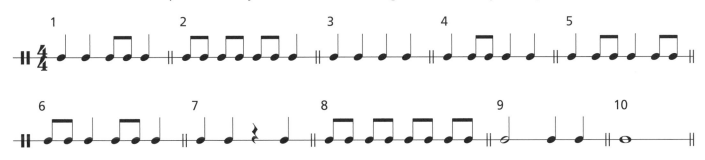

2 Use some of these to create your own four-bar rhythm. Clap the rhythm you compose, again counting four beats as you clap.

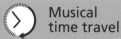
The Classical period

(about 1750–1810)

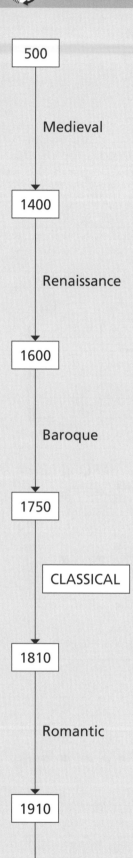

500

Medieval

1400

Renaissance

1600

Baroque

1750

CLASSICAL

1810

Romantic

1910

Contemporary

Look up the highlighted words to see what they mean.

Music became lighter and more elegant in the Classical period. Harmony was clear, and there was more emphasis on a graceful melody and accompaniment, with less use of counterpoint. There was greater variety and contrast within a piece, with a wider range of dynamics. The harpsichord was replaced by the pianoforte. The **clarinet**, invented at the start of the eighteenth century, grew in popularity. The orchestra became bigger and was led by a **conductor**.

Musical forms included the **symphony** (Haydn wrote at least 104!) and the solo concerto (Mozart wrote 21 for piano), which had a **cadenza**, where the soloist plays fast, often virtuosic music on their own. Important types of chamber music (smaller-scale instrumental pieces) were the **string quartet** and piano sonata. Vocal music saw the growth of **opera**, settings of the Mass and songs.

Composers: Joseph Haydn, Wolfgang Amadeus Mozart, Ludwig van Beethoven, Muzio Clementi, Christoph Gluck, C. P. E. Bach, J. C. Bach, Luigi Boccherini, Franz Schubert

Instruments: **pianoforte**, violin, viola, cello, double bass, flute, clarinet, oboe, bassoon, horns, trumpet, timpani

Online listening and sight-reading

The following themes are taken from well-known pieces of Classical music. Sight-read these, then listen to them online. Write a word to describe the character of each.

- Haydn, Trumpet Concerto in E flat major, first movement

  Character _____

- Mozart, *Eine kleine Nachtmusik* (Serenade, or 'A little night music'), first movement

  Character _____

20

Time piece

Das klinget so herrlich
(Classical period)

('That sounds so lovely') from the opera *The Magic Flute*

In this song, Papageno, the bird-catcher, plays his magic bells (on the glockenspiel) to charm and escape from the evil Monostatos and his slaves.

W. A. Mozart (1756–1791)
Arr. David Blackwell

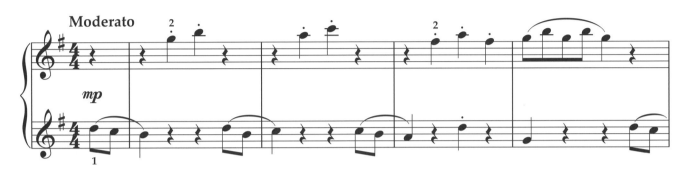

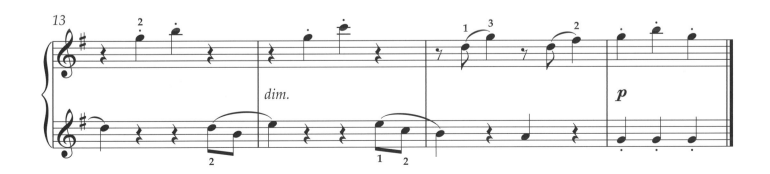

4 Melody and accompaniment

Being able to bring out the melody of a piece is an important skill. To do this, you must first spot the melody, and then have good independence of the hands, so one hand can play the accompaniment quietly while the other plays the melody louder. To make the melody louder than the accompaniment, practise each hand separately at the required dynamics; imagine the accompaniment as being as light as a feather and the melody louder like a ringing bell. Then memorise one part and focus on playing the other.

 Daily workouts

Five-finger Workout

Can you make one hand *forte*, the other *piano*, then swap around?

Balance Workout

Can you identify the melody and the accompaniment in this workout? Practise playing hands separately, with the melody *mf* and the accompaniment *p*, then put them together and bring out the melody.

Karen Marshall

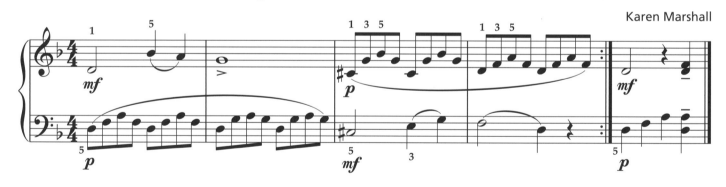

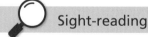 Sight-reading

Lavender's Blue

Can you identify the melody and accompaniment in this piece? Make the melody stronger than the accompaniment.

Traditional
Arr. David Blackwell

Sonatina in C

(Classical period)

Op. 36 No. 3, second movement

This piece has the melody in the right hand and the accompaniment in the left – be sure to bring out the melody clearly.

Can you write the meaning of the musical terms and dynamics in the boxes?

Muzio Clementi (1752–1832)

23

Writing a melody

Here is a nonsense rhyme by Edward Lear that we are going to use to create
a melody.

1 First say the rhyme in the rhythm shown and clap the pulse (two beats in
a bar, as marked).

2 Now improvise a tune to these words, using the notes of the pentatonic
scale (often used in folk songs). The notes of the scale are written below
in the treble and bass clefs. Experiment with different notes in your tune.
Repeated notes work well, as do notes next to each other (2nds), or missing
out a note (3rds).

3 Finally, write down your melody on this skeleton score. A few notes are
suggested, but use your own if you prefer!

Piano*Trainer*

Musical training

The harmonic minor scale generator

Using this scale generator, create the scales of A, E, D, G and B harmonic minor.

Name of scale _____

STEP 1

From the musical note names (A–G), select the notes in the correct order for the scale you want to play. Start with the key note and write them in the boxes (one or two octaves).

☐ ☐ ☐ ☐ ☐ ☐ ☐ ☐ ☐ ☐ ☐ ☐ ☐ ☐ ☐

STEP 2

The pattern of tones (T) and semitones (ST) for the **harmonic minor scale** is:

T ST T T ST T+½ ST

Check your letter names above – have you used the right pattern? Add any sharps or flats you need in the boxes. Play your scale through to check that it sounds right.

STEP 3

Write the letter names of the scale on the keyboard below, including any sharps or flats. Remember to use the correct pattern of tones and semitones.

Right-hand fingering:

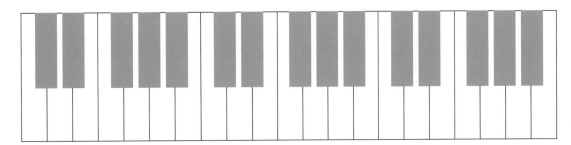

Left-hand fingering:

STEP 4

Work out the correct fingering – ask your teacher to help if necessary – and add the finger numbers to the keyboard above. Work out where your thumb goes first.

Common finger patterns

Right hand 1 2 3 1 2 3 4 1 2 3 1 2 3 4 5

Left hand 5 4 3 2 1 3 2 1 4 3 2 1 3 2 1 4 3 2 1 4 3 2 1 3 2 1 4 3 2 1

Karen Marshall

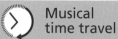

The Romantic period

(about 1810–1910)

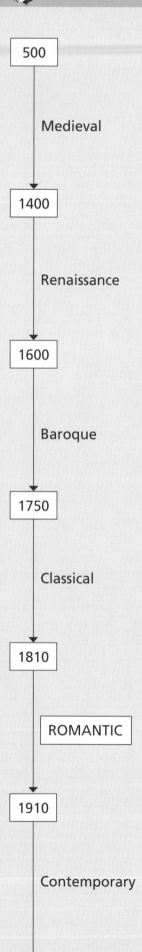

500

Medieval

1400

Renaissance

1600

Baroque

1750

Classical

1810

ROMANTIC

1910

Contemporary

Look up the highlighted words to see what they mean.

Music at this time became more expressive and communicated feelings and moods, such as joyfulness, mystery and adventure. It might draw inspiration from literature or art, or tell a story. The orchestra became bigger and more powerful, with new brass and percussion instruments added. Music was more dramatic, with a wide range of dynamics used.

Composition types included the **symphonic poem** (music telling a story, such as *The Sorcerer's Apprentice* by Dukas), incidental music (music written for a play, such as Mendelssohn's *A Midsummer Night's Dream*) and suites. Vocal music included opera, the Lied (a song) and **song cycles**. This period saw the rise of **nationalism** in music, when composers wrote music that represented their country, such as the polonaises of Chopin and Dvořák's *Slavonic Dances*.

Composers: Frédéric Chopin, Felix Mendelssohn, Hector Berlioz, Giuseppe Verdi, Johannes Brahms, Edvard Grieg, Richard Wagner, Franz Liszt, Pyotr Tchaikovsky, Antonin Dvořák, Jacques Offenbach, Léo Delibes, Edward Elgar

Instruments: all the instruments of the Classical orchestra and new ones such as the tuba, piccolo, contrabassoon, bass clarinet, **celeste** and xylophone

Online listening

In his operas, Wagner developed 'Leitmotifs', where a melody represents a particular character or theme. Here are two Leitmotifs from his opera cycle **Der Ring des Nibelungen** ('The Ring of the Nibelung'), a set of four operas with a linked story about a king stealing a ring from a dwarf. The first represents a sword and the second represents gold. Both include the same musical pattern – what type of pattern is it?

Later composers have used the same technique. Find out about these online:

- John Williams, music for the film *Star Wars* (The Force, Darth Vader, Princess Leia)
- Prokofiev, *Peter and the Wolf* (Peter, the Cat, the Duck, the Wolf, the Grandfather).

Flight of the Swans

(Romantic period)

from the ballet *Swan Lake*

This famous ballet tells the story of the princess Odette, who has been turned into a swan by an evil magician. In this scene, Odette and her flock of swans fly sadly across the sky.

Pyotr Ilyich Tchaikovsky (1840–1893)
Arr. David Blackwell

27

5 Part playing

and chord voicing

On the piano we can play different parts at the same time: we call this 'part playing'. In music, it's important to understand whether all the parts should be played with the same dynamics, or if some are more important and so need to be louder. When playing chords, try to make sure all the notes sound at the same time.

 Daily workout

Part Playing

Karen Marshall

 Sight-reading

Fidgety Fingers

Make sure you play the notes in the chords together.

David Blackwell

Duet part

Repertoire

The Industrious Student

(Romantic period)

Op. 31 No. 3

Notice the three parts in the first section: one part in the right hand and two parts in the left hand. Play each of these parts on their own, then practise parts 1 and 3 together, 2 and 3 together, and 1 and 2 together.

Kaspar Jakob Bischoff (1823–1893)

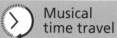

The Contemporary period

(1910 to the present day)

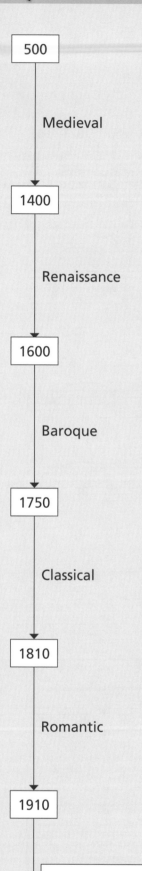

500

Medieval

1400

Renaissance

1600

Baroque

1750

Classical

1810

Romantic

1910

CONTEMPORARY

Look up the highlighted words to see what they mean.

In the twentieth century the idea of tonality – music that is in keys – broke down. Music became more dissonant or 'atonal' (without a key) or bitonal (in two keys at the same time). Stravinsky's ballet *The Rite of Spring* caused a riot at its premiere in 1913. Shortly afterwards, Schoenberg developed the concept of **serialism** (twelve-tone technique), where all 12 semitones of the octave are of equal importance. Music was also composed in many different styles: some composers took inspiration from folk music (Vaughan Williams and Bartók), and some broke the 12 semitones of the octave into even smaller units (**microtonal music**). In **electronic music** composers used electronic instruments and sound technology in their pieces, while in **minimalism** composers created simpler pieces that repeated musical ideas and phrases.

Alongside these forms were the many types of popular music, including blues, jazz, rock and roll, disco, pop, and many others. There was also interest in **world music**, the performance of traditional musics from around the world. Music in film became very important, adding much to the atmosphere and character of the action on screen.

Composers: Debussy, Sibelius, Vaughan Williams, Stravinsky, Bartók, Schoenberg, Copland, Gershwin, Shostakovich, Prokofiev, Villa-Lobos, Messiaen, Britten, Steve Reich, Ligeti, Arvo Pärt, John Williams, Hans Zimmer

Instruments and equipment: saxophone, synthesizer, loop stations, electric guitars, microphones, drum machines

Online listening
Listen to these pieces and describe their character:

* Arnold Schoenberg: 'Mondestrunken' from *Pierrot Lunaire*: an atonal song.

  Character _____

  _____

* Steve Reich: *Clapping Music*, a minimalist piece where performers clap an intricate pattern.

  Character _____

  _____

* Hans Zimmer: 'He's a Pirate' from the film *Pirates of the Caribbean*.

  Character _____

  _____

Time piece

Mars, The Bringer of War

(20th century)

from *The Planets*

Holst's orchestral suite *The Planets* was written in 1914–16. Its seven movements describe the character of the seven planets known at the time and how they influence life on Earth. The rhythm of the left hand is very important in this piece – imagine it to these words:

Be on your guard for here comes Mars!

Gustav Holst (1874–1934)
Arr. David Blackwell

Menacingly

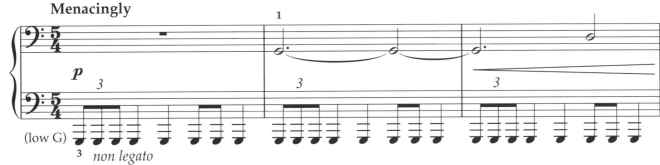

Musical training

Getting to know chords

There are lots of triads to identify in this piece – can you find the chords listed below? Use the boxes provided to identify them.

Root position chords: D minor, D major and F major;
C major 1st inversion, A major 2nd inversion

Describe the following:

a root position chord _____

1st inversion _____

2nd inversion _____

Repertoire

Gypsy Dance

(Classical period)

Joseph Haydn (1732–1809)

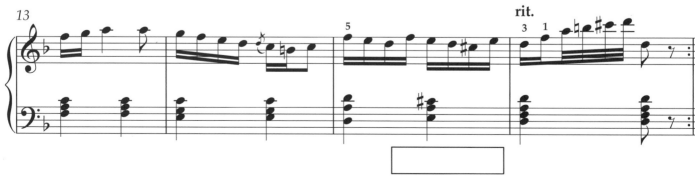